50 Historical Recipes Revived for Home

By: Kelly Johnson

Table of Contents

- Beef Wellington
- Beef Stroganoff
- Chicken à la King
- Chicken Tetrazzini
- Chateaubriand
- Coq au Vin
- Crab Louie Salad
- Croque Monsieur
- Eggs Benedict
- Escargot
- Gâteau Saint-Honoré
- Lobster Newberg
- Oysters Rockefeller
- Peking Duck
- Quiche Lorraine
- Ratatouille
- Salisbury Steak
- Shrimp Scampi
- Sole Meunière
- Steak Diane
- Tournedos Rossini
- Waldorf Salad
- Welsh Rarebit
- Beef Burgundy
- Bouillabaisse
- Chicken Marengo
- Chicken Cordon Bleu
- Coquilles St. Jacques
- Crêpes Suzette
- Duck à l'Orange
- Eggs à la Goldenrod
- Lobster Thermidor
- Oysters Bienville
- Peach Melba
- Pheasant à la Kiev

- Potage Parmentier (Potato Leek Soup)
- Quenelles de Brochet
- Rabbit Stew
- Sauerbraten
- Shrimp Cocktail
- Sole Veronique
- Steak Tartare
- Tarte Tatin
- Terrine de Foie Gras
- Tomato Aspic
- Trout Almondine
- Veal Oscar
- Veal Piccata
- Wiener Schnitzel
- Yorkshire Pudding

Beef Wellington

Ingredients:

- 1 whole beef tenderloin (about 2 pounds)
- Salt and pepper, to taste
- 2 tablespoons olive oil
- 1/2 pound mushrooms, finely chopped
- 2 shallots, finely chopped
- 2 cloves garlic, minced
- 2 tablespoons butter
- 2 tablespoons fresh parsley, chopped
- 1 sheet puff pastry, thawed if frozen
- 1 egg, beaten (for egg wash)

Instructions:

1. Preheat your oven to 400°F (200°C).
2. Season the beef tenderloin generously with salt and pepper.
3. Heat the olive oil in a skillet over medium-high heat. Sear the beef tenderloin on all sides until browned, about 2 minutes per side. Remove from the skillet and set aside to cool.
4. In the same skillet, melt the butter over medium heat. Add the chopped mushrooms, shallots, and garlic. Cook until the mushrooms release their moisture and the mixture becomes dry, about 8-10 minutes. Stir in the chopped parsley and season with salt and pepper to taste. Remove from heat and let cool slightly.
5. Roll out the puff pastry on a lightly floured surface to a rectangle large enough to wrap around the beef tenderloin.
6. Spread the mushroom mixture evenly over the puff pastry, leaving a border around the edges.
7. Place the seared beef tenderloin on top of the mushroom mixture.
8. Carefully fold the puff pastry over the beef, sealing the edges and trimming any excess pastry.
9. Place the Beef Wellington seam-side down on a baking sheet lined with parchment paper.
10. Brush the top and sides of the pastry with the beaten egg to create a golden finish.

11. Using a sharp knife, make a few slits in the top of the pastry to allow steam to escape.
12. Bake in the preheated oven for 35-40 minutes, or until the pastry is golden brown and the internal temperature of the beef reaches your desired level of doneness (135°F / 57°C for medium-rare).
13. Remove from the oven and let rest for 10 minutes before slicing and serving.

Beef Wellington is often served with a side of mashed potatoes, roasted vegetables, or a simple green salad. Enjoy this elegant and flavorful dish!

Beef Stroganoff

Ingredients:

- 1 pound beef sirloin or tenderloin, sliced thinly against the grain
- Salt and pepper, to taste
- 2 tablespoons olive oil
- 1 onion, finely chopped
- 2 cloves garlic, minced
- 8 ounces mushrooms, sliced
- 2 tablespoons all-purpose flour
- 1 cup beef broth
- 1 tablespoon Dijon mustard
- 2 tablespoons Worcestershire sauce
- 1 cup sour cream
- Fresh parsley, chopped, for garnish
- Cooked egg noodles or rice, for serving

Instructions:

1. Season the sliced beef with salt and pepper to taste.
2. Heat the olive oil in a large skillet over medium-high heat. Add the beef slices in batches and cook until browned on all sides. Remove the beef from the skillet and set aside.
3. In the same skillet, add the chopped onion and cook until softened, about 3-4 minutes. Add the minced garlic and cook for an additional 1 minute.
4. Add the sliced mushrooms to the skillet and cook until they release their moisture and become tender, about 5-6 minutes.
5. Sprinkle the flour over the mushrooms and stir to coat evenly. Cook for 1-2 minutes to remove the raw flour taste.
6. Slowly pour in the beef broth, stirring constantly to prevent lumps from forming. Bring the mixture to a simmer.
7. Stir in the Dijon mustard and Worcestershire sauce, then return the cooked beef slices to the skillet. Cook for an additional 2-3 minutes, allowing the flavors to meld.
8. Reduce the heat to low and stir in the sour cream until the sauce is smooth and creamy. Be careful not to let the sauce boil once the sour cream is added to prevent curdling.

9. Taste and adjust seasoning with salt and pepper if needed.
10. Serve the Beef Stroganoff hot over cooked egg noodles or rice, garnished with chopped parsley.

Beef Stroganoff pairs well with a side of steamed vegetables or a crisp green salad.

Enjoy this comforting and flavorful dish!

Chicken à la King

Ingredients:

- 2 tablespoons unsalted butter
- 1 onion, finely chopped
- 1 red bell pepper, diced
- 1 green bell pepper, diced
- 8 ounces mushrooms, sliced
- 1/4 cup all-purpose flour
- 2 cups chicken broth
- 1 cup heavy cream
- 2 cups cooked chicken, diced or shredded
- Salt and pepper, to taste
- 1/4 cup chopped fresh parsley
- Toast, rice, or puff pastry, for serving

Instructions:

1. In a large skillet or saucepan, melt the butter over medium heat. Add the chopped onion and diced bell peppers, and cook until softened, about 5 minutes.
2. Add the sliced mushrooms to the skillet and cook until they release their moisture and become tender, about 5-6 minutes.
3. Sprinkle the flour over the vegetables in the skillet and stir to coat evenly. Cook for 1-2 minutes to remove the raw flour taste.
4. Slowly pour in the chicken broth, stirring constantly to prevent lumps from forming. Bring the mixture to a simmer.
5. Stir in the heavy cream and continue to simmer until the sauce thickens, about 5 minutes.
6. Add the cooked chicken to the skillet and stir to combine. Cook for an additional 2-3 minutes, until the chicken is heated through.
7. Season the Chicken à la King with salt and pepper to taste. Stir in the chopped parsley just before serving.
8. Serve the Chicken à la King hot over toast, rice, or puff pastry.

Chicken à la King is often garnished with additional parsley and served with a side of steamed vegetables or a green salad. Enjoy this comforting and flavorful dish!

Chicken Tetrazzini

Ingredients:

- 8 ounces spaghetti or fettuccine pasta
- 2 tablespoons unsalted butter
- 1 onion, finely chopped
- 8 ounces mushrooms, sliced
- 2 cloves garlic, minced
- 1/4 cup all-purpose flour
- 2 cups chicken broth
- 1 cup heavy cream
- 1/2 cup grated Parmesan cheese
- 2 cups cooked chicken, diced or shredded
- Salt and pepper, to taste
- 1/4 cup chopped fresh parsley
- 1/2 cup grated mozzarella cheese

Instructions:

1. Preheat your oven to 375°F (190°C). Grease a 9x13-inch baking dish and set aside.
2. Cook the pasta according to the package instructions until al dente. Drain and set aside.
3. In a large skillet or saucepan, melt the butter over medium heat. Add the chopped onion and cook until softened, about 5 minutes.
4. Add the sliced mushrooms to the skillet and cook until they release their moisture and become tender, about 5-6 minutes.
5. Stir in the minced garlic and cook for an additional 1 minute.
6. Sprinkle the flour over the vegetables in the skillet and stir to coat evenly. Cook for 1-2 minutes to remove the raw flour taste.
7. Slowly pour in the chicken broth, stirring constantly to prevent lumps from forming. Bring the mixture to a simmer.
8. Stir in the heavy cream and grated Parmesan cheese. Continue to simmer until the sauce thickens, about 5 minutes.
9. Add the cooked chicken and cooked pasta to the skillet, stirring until everything is well coated in the sauce. Season with salt and pepper to taste.
10. Transfer the mixture to the prepared baking dish, spreading it out evenly.

11. Sprinkle the grated mozzarella cheese over the top of the casserole.
12. Bake in the preheated oven for 25-30 minutes, or until the cheese is melted and bubbly and the casserole is heated through.
13. Remove from the oven and let it rest for a few minutes before serving.
14. Garnish with chopped parsley before serving.

Chicken Tetrazzini is often served with a side of garlic bread or a green salad. Enjoy this comforting and flavorful dish!

Chateaubriand

Ingredients:

- 1 1/2 to 2 pounds beef tenderloin, center-cut, trimmed and tied
- Salt and pepper, to taste
- 2 tablespoons olive oil
- 2 tablespoons unsalted butter
- 2 shallots, finely chopped
- 1/4 cup brandy or cognac
- 1 cup beef broth
- 1/2 cup heavy cream
- 2 teaspoons Dijon mustard
- 1 tablespoon fresh parsley, chopped (for garnish)

Instructions:

1. Preheat your oven to 400°F (200°C).
2. Season the beef tenderloin generously with salt and pepper on all sides.
3. Heat the olive oil in an oven-proof skillet over high heat. Once hot, add the beef tenderloin and sear on all sides until well-browned, about 2 minutes per side.
4. Transfer the skillet to the preheated oven and roast the beef tenderloin until it reaches your desired level of doneness. For medium-rare, roast for about 15-20 minutes, or until the internal temperature reaches 135°F (57°C) when measured with a meat thermometer inserted into the thickest part of the steak. Adjust cooking time for your preferred level of doneness.
5. Once the beef is cooked to your liking, remove it from the oven and transfer it to a cutting board. Tent loosely with foil and let it rest for 10 minutes before slicing.
6. While the beef is resting, make the sauce. In the same skillet used to cook the beef, melt the butter over medium heat. Add the chopped shallots and cook until softened, about 2-3 minutes.
7. Carefully add the brandy or cognac to the skillet and cook, stirring, until it has mostly evaporated.
8. Pour in the beef broth and bring the mixture to a simmer. Let it cook until slightly reduced, about 5 minutes.
9. Stir in the heavy cream and Dijon mustard, and continue to simmer until the sauce thickens slightly, about 3-4 minutes.
10. Season the sauce with salt and pepper to taste.

11. To serve, slice the rested beef tenderloin into thick slices and arrange on a serving platter. Pour the sauce over the top, and garnish with chopped parsley.
12. Serve the Chateaubriand with your choice of side dishes, such as roasted potatoes, steamed vegetables, or a green salad.

Enjoy this elegant and flavorful French dish!

Coq au Vin

Ingredients:

- 1 whole chicken, cut into 8 pieces (or use chicken thighs and drumsticks)
- Salt and pepper, to taste
- 4 ounces bacon, diced
- 2 tablespoons unsalted butter
- 10-12 small pearl onions, peeled
- 8 ounces mushrooms, quartered
- 3 cloves garlic, minced
- 2 tablespoons all-purpose flour
- 2 cups red wine (such as Burgundy, Pinot Noir, or Merlot)
- 1 cup chicken broth
- 2 tablespoons tomato paste
- 2 bay leaves
- 2 sprigs fresh thyme
- Chopped fresh parsley, for garnish

Instructions:

1. Season the chicken pieces with salt and pepper.
2. In a large Dutch oven or heavy-bottomed pot, cook the diced bacon over medium heat until crispy. Remove the bacon with a slotted spoon and set aside, leaving the bacon fat in the pot.
3. Add the butter to the pot. Once melted, add the chicken pieces in batches and brown them on all sides. Remove the chicken from the pot and set aside.
4. In the same pot, add the pearl onions and mushrooms. Cook, stirring occasionally, until they are golden brown, about 5-7 minutes.
5. Add the minced garlic to the pot and cook for an additional minute.
6. Sprinkle the flour over the vegetables in the pot and stir to coat evenly. Cook for 1-2 minutes to remove the raw flour taste.
7. Slowly pour in the red wine and chicken broth, stirring constantly to incorporate. Add the tomato paste, bay leaves, and thyme sprigs. Bring the mixture to a simmer.
8. Return the browned chicken pieces and cooked bacon to the pot. Cover and simmer over low heat for 1 to 1 1/2 hours, or until the chicken is tender and cooked through, and the sauce has thickened.
9. Taste and adjust seasoning with salt and pepper if needed.

10. Serve the Coq au Vin hot, garnished with chopped fresh parsley. It pairs well with mashed potatoes, crusty bread, or rice.

Enjoy this rich and flavorful French classic!

Crab Louie Salad

Ingredients for Salad:

- 1 pound lump crab meat, picked over for shells
- 1 head iceberg lettuce, chopped
- 2 tomatoes, sliced
- 2 hard-boiled eggs, sliced
- 1 cucumber, sliced
- 1 avocado, sliced
- 1 cup cooked asparagus spears, chilled
- 1 cup cooked artichoke hearts, chilled
- Lemon wedges, for garnish
- Fresh parsley, chopped, for garnish
- Salt and pepper, to taste

Ingredients for Dressing:

- 1 cup mayonnaise
- 1/4 cup ketchup
- 2 tablespoons fresh lemon juice
- 1 tablespoon Worcestershire sauce
- 1 tablespoon prepared horseradish
- 1 teaspoon Dijon mustard
- Salt and pepper, to taste

Instructions:

1. In a large mixing bowl, combine the chopped iceberg lettuce, sliced tomatoes, sliced cucumber, sliced avocado, cooked asparagus spears, and cooked artichoke hearts. Toss gently to combine.
2. Arrange the crab meat on top of the salad mixture.
3. In a small bowl, prepare the dressing by whisking together the mayonnaise, ketchup, fresh lemon juice, Worcestershire sauce, prepared horseradish, and Dijon mustard until smooth. Season with salt and pepper to taste.
4. Drizzle the dressing over the Crab Louie Salad or serve it on the side.
5. Garnish the salad with slices of hard-boiled eggs, lemon wedges, and chopped fresh parsley.

6. Serve the Crab Louie Salad immediately, accompanied by crusty bread or crackers, if desired.

Enjoy this refreshing and flavorful salad as a light meal or appetizer!

Croque Monsieur

Ingredients:

- 8 slices of good-quality sandwich bread (such as sourdough or country loaf)
- 8 slices of cooked ham
- 8 slices of Gruyère or Emmental cheese
- 2 tablespoons unsalted butter
- 2 tablespoons all-purpose flour
- 1 cup milk
- 1/4 teaspoon ground nutmeg
- Salt and pepper, to taste
- Dijon mustard, for spreading (optional)
- Additional butter, for spreading on the bread

Instructions:

1. Preheat your oven to 375°F (190°C). Line a baking sheet with parchment paper.
2. To make the béchamel sauce, melt the butter in a saucepan over medium heat. Once melted, whisk in the flour to form a smooth paste (roux). Cook the roux, stirring constantly, for 1-2 minutes to cook off the raw flour taste.
3. Gradually pour in the milk while whisking constantly to prevent lumps from forming. Continue to whisk until the sauce thickens and becomes smooth, about 3-5 minutes.
4. Stir in the ground nutmeg and season with salt and pepper to taste. Remove the sauce from the heat and set aside.
5. If using Dijon mustard, spread a thin layer on half of the bread slices.
6. Place a slice of ham and a slice of cheese on top of each mustard-coated bread slice.
7. Top each ham and cheese slice with another slice of bread to form sandwiches.
8. Spread a thin layer of butter on the outside of each sandwich.
9. Place the sandwiches on the prepared baking sheet and bake in the preheated oven for 10-15 minutes, or until the bread is golden and the cheese is melted and bubbly.
10. Remove the sandwiches from the oven and carefully transfer them to serving plates.
11. Spoon the prepared béchamel sauce over the top of each sandwich.

12. Serve the Croque Monsieur sandwiches hot, accompanied by a simple green salad or pickles, if desired.

Enjoy these indulgent and delicious French sandwiches for a satisfying meal or snack!

Eggs Benedict

Ingredients:

- 4 large eggs
- 2 English muffins, split and toasted
- 4 slices Canadian bacon or cooked ham
- Hollandaise sauce (see recipe below)
- Chopped fresh chives or parsley, for garnish (optional)

Instructions:

1. Prepare the hollandaise sauce according to the recipe below and keep it warm.
2. In a large skillet, heat a small amount of oil or butter over medium heat. Add the Canadian bacon slices and cook until heated through and lightly browned on both sides. Remove from the skillet and keep warm.
3. To poach the eggs, bring a large pot of water to a gentle simmer. Crack each egg into a small bowl or cup. Using a spoon, create a whirlpool in the simmering water and gently slide the eggs, one at a time, into the center of the whirlpool. Cook for about 3-4 minutes for soft-poached eggs or longer if desired. Use a slotted spoon to carefully remove the poached eggs from the water and drain on a paper towel.
4. To assemble the Eggs Benedict, place a toasted English muffin half on each serving plate. Top each half with a slice of Canadian bacon or ham.
5. Carefully place a poached egg on top of each Canadian bacon slice.
6. Spoon hollandaise sauce generously over each poached egg.
7. Garnish with chopped fresh chives or parsley, if desired.
8. Serve the Eggs Benedict immediately, while still warm.

Hollandaise Sauce:

Ingredients:

- 3 large egg yolks
- 1 tablespoon lemon juice
- 1/2 cup unsalted butter, melted
- Pinch of cayenne pepper
- Salt, to taste

Instructions:

1. In a heatproof bowl set over a pot of simmering water (double boiler method), whisk together the egg yolks and lemon juice until pale and slightly thickened.
2. Gradually drizzle in the melted butter while whisking constantly, until the sauce thickens and emulsifies.
3. Remove the bowl from the heat and stir in the cayenne pepper and salt to taste.
4. Keep the hollandaise sauce warm until ready to serve, stirring occasionally to prevent a skin from forming.

Enjoy this classic brunch favorite!

Escargot

Ingredients:
- 24 large canned escargot
- 1/2 cup unsalted butter, softened
- 2 cloves garlic, minced
- 2 tablespoons fresh parsley, finely chopped
- 1 tablespoon fresh lemon juice
- Salt and pepper, to taste
- 12 small escargot shells
- Baguette or French bread, for serving

Instructions:

1. Preheat your oven to 400°F (200°C).
2. Rinse the canned escargot under cold water and drain well.
3. In a small mixing bowl, combine the softened butter, minced garlic, chopped parsley, and lemon juice. Season with salt and pepper to taste. Mix until well combined.
4. Place a small amount of the garlic parsley butter in each of the 12 escargot shells.
5. Add two escargot to each shell on top of the butter.
6. Place the filled shells in an escargot dish or a baking dish with indentations to hold the shells upright.
7. Bake in the preheated oven for 10-12 minutes, or until the butter is bubbling and the escargot are heated through.
8. While the escargot are baking, slice the baguette or French bread into thin slices.
9. Once the escargot are cooked, remove them from the oven and serve immediately, accompanied by the slices of bread for dipping into the garlic parsley butter.

Enjoy this luxurious and flavorful French appetizer with a glass of white wine!

Gâteau Saint-Honoré

Ingredients:

For the Puff Pastry:

- 1 sheet of store-bought puff pastry or homemade puff pastry

For the Choux Pastry:

- 1/2 cup water
- 1/4 cup unsalted butter
- 1/4 teaspoon salt
- 1/2 cup all-purpose flour
- 2 large eggs

For the Pastry Cream:

- 1 cup whole milk
- 4 large egg yolks
- 1/4 cup granulated sugar
- 2 tablespoons cornstarch
- 1 teaspoon vanilla extract

For the Whipped Cream:

- 1 cup heavy cream
- 2 tablespoons powdered sugar
- 1 teaspoon vanilla extract

For Assembly:

- Granulated sugar, for caramelizing
- Fresh berries or fruit, for garnish (optional)

Instructions:

1. Preheat your oven to 400°F (200°C).
2. Prepare the puff pastry: Roll out the puff pastry sheet to about 1/4 inch thickness. Use a round pastry cutter to cut out circles slightly smaller than the

diameter of your tartlet molds. Place the puff pastry circles on a parchment-lined baking sheet and chill in the refrigerator while you prepare the choux pastry.

3. Prepare the choux pastry: In a saucepan, combine the water, butter, and salt. Bring to a boil over medium heat. Remove from heat and quickly stir in the flour until well combined. Return the saucepan to low heat and cook the mixture, stirring constantly, for about 1-2 minutes until it forms a smooth ball of dough and leaves a thin film on the bottom of the pan.
4. Transfer the choux pastry dough to a mixing bowl and let it cool slightly. Gradually add the eggs, one at a time, beating well after each addition, until the dough is smooth and shiny.
5. Transfer the choux pastry dough to a piping bag fitted with a large round tip. Pipe a ring of choux pastry onto each puff pastry circle, leaving the center open.
6. Bake the pastry shells in the preheated oven for 20-25 minutes, or until golden brown and puffed. Remove from the oven and let cool completely.
7. Prepare the pastry cream: In a saucepan, heat the milk until steaming but not boiling. In a separate bowl, whisk together the egg yolks, sugar, and cornstarch until smooth and pale yellow. Gradually pour the hot milk into the egg mixture, whisking constantly.
8. Return the mixture to the saucepan and cook over medium heat, stirring constantly, until thickened. Remove from heat and stir in the vanilla extract. Transfer the pastry cream to a bowl and cover the surface with plastic wrap to prevent a skin from forming. Chill in the refrigerator until cold.
9. Prepare the whipped cream: In a mixing bowl, beat the heavy cream, powdered sugar, and vanilla extract until stiff peaks form.
10. Assemble the Gâteau Saint-Honoré: Fill the center of each pastry shell with pastry cream. Pipe or spoon a ring of whipped cream around the edge of each pastry shell.
11. Sprinkle granulated sugar over the whipped cream and use a kitchen torch to caramelize the sugar until golden brown.
12. Garnish with fresh berries or fruit, if desired.
13. Serve the Gâteau Saint-Honoré immediately or refrigerate until ready to serve.

Enjoy this elegant and decadent French dessert!

Lobster Newberg

Ingredients:

- 2 lobsters (about 1 1/2 to 2 pounds each), cooked and meat removed from shells
- 4 tablespoons unsalted butter
- 1/4 cup brandy or dry sherry
- 1 cup heavy cream
- 4 large egg yolks
- Salt and pepper, to taste
- Pinch of cayenne pepper (optional)
- Chopped fresh parsley, for garnish
- Toasted bread or puff pastry shells, for serving

Instructions:

1. Cut the lobster meat into bite-sized pieces.
2. In a large skillet or sauté pan, melt the butter over medium heat.
3. Add the lobster meat to the skillet and cook briefly, just until heated through, about 2-3 minutes.
4. Carefully add the brandy or sherry to the skillet and cook for another 2-3 minutes, allowing the alcohol to evaporate.
5. Reduce the heat to low and pour in the heavy cream. Stir gently to combine with the lobster and simmer for 2-3 minutes.
6. In a small bowl, whisk together the egg yolks. Gradually add a small amount of the hot cream mixture to the egg yolks, whisking constantly to temper the yolks and prevent them from curdling.
7. Slowly pour the egg yolk mixture back into the skillet, stirring constantly, and cook until the sauce thickens slightly, about 2-3 minutes. Be careful not to let the sauce boil to avoid curdling.
8. Season the sauce with salt, pepper, and a pinch of cayenne pepper, if using. Taste and adjust seasoning as needed.
9. Remove the skillet from heat and garnish with chopped fresh parsley.
10. Serve the Lobster Newberg hot, spooned over toasted bread or puff pastry shells.

Enjoy this decadent and flavorful seafood dish as a special treat for a special occasion!

Oysters Rockefeller

Ingredients:

- 24 fresh oysters, shucked, with their shells reserved
- 1/2 cup unsalted butter
- 1/2 cup finely chopped shallots
- 1/2 cup finely chopped celery
- 1/2 cup finely chopped green bell pepper
- 2 cloves garlic, minced
- 1 cup fresh spinach leaves, chopped
- 1/2 cup fresh parsley leaves, chopped
- 1/4 cup Pernod or other anise-flavored liqueur (optional)
- 1/2 cup breadcrumbs
- 1/4 cup grated Parmesan cheese
- Salt and pepper, to taste
- Rock salt or coarse salt, for serving (optional)
- Lemon wedges, for serving

Instructions:

1. Preheat your oven to 450°F (230°C).
2. Clean the reserved oyster shells and arrange them on a baking sheet lined with parchment paper or rock salt (to help stabilize them).
3. In a large skillet, melt the butter over medium heat. Add the chopped shallots, celery, and green bell pepper, and cook until softened, about 5-7 minutes.
4. Add the minced garlic to the skillet and cook for an additional minute.
5. Stir in the chopped spinach and parsley, and cook until wilted, about 2-3 minutes.
6. If using, add the Pernod or anise-flavored liqueur to the skillet and cook for another minute to allow the alcohol to evaporate.
7. Remove the skillet from heat and stir in the breadcrumbs and grated Parmesan cheese. Season with salt and pepper to taste.
8. Place a spoonful of the spinach mixture on top of each shucked oyster in its shell.
9. Bake the Oysters Rockefeller in the preheated oven for 8-10 minutes, or until the topping is golden and bubbly.
10. Remove from the oven and let cool slightly before serving.

11. Serve the Oysters Rockefeller hot, arranged on a platter with lemon wedges on the side.

Enjoy these elegant and flavorful oysters as a decadent appetizer or part of a special meal!

Peking Duck

Ingredients:

- 1 whole duck (about 5-6 pounds)
- 1 tablespoon Chinese five-spice powder
- 2 tablespoons honey
- 2 tablespoons soy sauce
- 1 tablespoon rice vinegar
- 1 teaspoon sesame oil
- 2 tablespoons maltose or honey (for glazing)
- Thin pancakes (store-bought or homemade)
- Hoisin sauce, for serving
- Thinly sliced spring onions (scallions), for serving
- Thinly sliced cucumber, for serving

Instructions:

1. Begin by preparing the duck. Rinse the duck inside and out under cold water and pat it dry with paper towels.
2. Mix together the Chinese five-spice powder, honey, soy sauce, rice vinegar, and sesame oil to make a marinade.
3. Rub the marinade all over the duck, inside and out, ensuring it is evenly coated. Allow the duck to marinate for at least 4 hours, or preferably overnight in the refrigerator, covered.
4. Preheat your oven to 375°F (190°C).
5. Remove the duck from the refrigerator and let it come to room temperature for about 30 minutes before cooking.
6. Place the duck on a roasting rack set over a baking tray, breast-side up. Truss the duck if desired.
7. Roast the duck in the preheated oven for about 1.5 to 2 hours, or until the skin is golden brown and crispy and the internal temperature reaches 165°F (74°C) in the thickest part of the thigh.
8. While the duck is roasting, prepare the glaze by heating the maltose or honey in a small saucepan until it becomes liquid and slightly runny.
9. Brush the glaze over the duck during the last 20-30 minutes of cooking, basting it several times to achieve a shiny finish.

10. Once the duck is cooked, remove it from the oven and let it rest for about 15-20 minutes before carving.
11. To serve, carve the duck into thin slices, including both the skin and meat.
12. Serve the sliced duck with thin pancakes, hoisin sauce, sliced spring onions, and sliced cucumber. To assemble, spread hoisin sauce onto a pancake, add slices of duck, spring onions, and cucumber, then roll it up and enjoy!

Peking Duck is a delightful and flavorful dish that's perfect for special occasions or a festive meal with family and friends. Enjoy the crispy skin and tender meat alongside the savory and sweet accompaniments!

Quiche Lorraine

Ingredients:

For the Pastry Crust:

- 1 1/4 cups all-purpose flour
- 1/2 teaspoon salt
- 1/2 cup cold unsalted butter, cut into small cubes
- 3-4 tablespoons ice water

For the Filling:

- 6 slices bacon, diced
- 1 cup shredded Gruyère or Swiss cheese
- 4 large eggs
- 1 cup heavy cream
- 1/2 cup whole milk
- 1/4 teaspoon salt
- 1/4 teaspoon black pepper
- Pinch of ground nutmeg

Instructions:

1. Preheat your oven to 375°F (190°C).
2. Prepare the pastry crust:
    - In a large mixing bowl, combine the flour and salt. Add the cold butter cubes and use a pastry cutter or your fingertips to work the butter into the flour until the mixture resembles coarse crumbs.
    - Gradually add the ice water, 1 tablespoon at a time, mixing gently with a fork, until the dough comes together. Be careful not to overwork the dough.
    - Shape the dough into a disk, wrap it in plastic wrap, and refrigerate for at least 30 minutes.
3. Roll out the chilled pastry dough on a lightly floured surface to fit a 9-inch tart or pie pan. Press the dough into the pan, trimming any excess, and prick the bottom with a fork. Line the crust with parchment paper or aluminum foil and fill it with pie weights or dried beans.

4. Blind bake the crust in the preheated oven for 15 minutes. Remove the parchment paper and pie weights, and bake for an additional 5 minutes, or until the crust is lightly golden. Remove from the oven and let cool slightly.
5. In a skillet, cook the diced bacon over medium heat until crispy. Remove from the skillet and drain on paper towels.
6. Sprinkle the cooked bacon and shredded cheese evenly over the bottom of the partially baked pastry crust.
7. In a mixing bowl, whisk together the eggs, heavy cream, milk, salt, pepper, and nutmeg until well combined.
8. Pour the egg mixture over the bacon and cheese in the pastry crust.
9. Bake the quiche in the preheated oven for 30-35 minutes, or until the filling is set and the top is golden brown.
10. Remove from the oven and let the quiche cool for a few minutes before slicing.
11. Serve the Quiche Lorraine warm or at room temperature, accompanied by a crisp green salad or your favorite side dishes.

Enjoy this classic French dish as a delicious brunch or light lunch option!

Ratatouille

Ingredients:

- 2 tablespoons olive oil
- 1 onion, diced
- 2 cloves garlic, minced
- 1 eggplant, diced
- 2 zucchinis, diced
- 2 bell peppers (red, yellow, or green), diced
- 4 tomatoes, diced (or 1 can of diced tomatoes)
- 1 tablespoon tomato paste
- 1 teaspoon dried thyme
- 1 teaspoon dried oregano
- Salt and pepper, to taste
- Fresh basil leaves, chopped, for garnish (optional)

Instructions:

1. Heat the olive oil in a large skillet or Dutch oven over medium heat.
2. Add the diced onion to the skillet and cook until softened, about 5 minutes.
3. Add the minced garlic to the skillet and cook for an additional minute, until fragrant.
4. Add the diced eggplant to the skillet and cook for about 5 minutes, until it begins to soften.
5. Stir in the diced zucchini and bell peppers, and cook for another 5 minutes, until the vegetables are slightly tender.
6. Add the diced tomatoes, tomato paste, dried thyme, and dried oregano to the skillet. Season with salt and pepper to taste.
7. Stir well to combine all the ingredients. Reduce the heat to low, cover, and let the ratatouille simmer for about 20-25 minutes, stirring occasionally, until the vegetables are cooked through and the flavors meld together.
8. Taste and adjust seasoning if needed.
9. Remove the skillet from heat and let the ratatouille rest for a few minutes before serving.
10. Serve the ratatouille hot, garnished with chopped fresh basil leaves if desired.

Ratatouille can be enjoyed as a side dish, served over rice or couscous, or as a main course with crusty bread. It's a versatile and comforting dish that's perfect for showcasing seasonal vegetables and Mediterranean flavors.

Salisbury Steak

Ingredients:

For the Salisbury Steak:

- 1 pound ground beef (preferably lean)
- 1/2 cup breadcrumbs
- 1/4 cup finely chopped onion
- 1 clove garlic, minced
- 1 large egg
- 1 tablespoon Worcestershire sauce
- 1 teaspoon Dijon mustard
- 1/2 teaspoon salt
- 1/4 teaspoon black pepper
- 1 tablespoon olive oil, for cooking

For the Mushroom Gravy:

- 1 tablespoon butter
- 8 ounces mushrooms, sliced
- 1/4 cup finely chopped onion
- 2 cloves garlic, minced
- 2 tablespoons all-purpose flour
- 2 cups beef broth
- 1 tablespoon Worcestershire sauce
- Salt and pepper, to taste
- Chopped fresh parsley, for garnish (optional)

Instructions:

1. In a large mixing bowl, combine the ground beef, breadcrumbs, finely chopped onion, minced garlic, egg, Worcestershire sauce, Dijon mustard, salt, and pepper. Mix until well combined.
2. Divide the beef mixture into 4 equal portions and shape each portion into an oval-shaped patty, about 1/2 inch thick.

3. Heat the olive oil in a large skillet over medium-high heat. Once hot, add the beef patties to the skillet and cook for 4-5 minutes on each side, or until browned and cooked through. Remove the patties from the skillet and set aside.
4. In the same skillet, melt the butter over medium heat. Add the sliced mushrooms and cook until they release their moisture and start to brown, about 5-7 minutes.
5. Add the finely chopped onion and minced garlic to the skillet with the mushrooms, and cook for an additional 2-3 minutes, until the onion is softened and the garlic is fragrant.
6. Sprinkle the flour over the mushrooms and onions in the skillet, and stir to coat evenly. Cook for 1-2 minutes to cook off the raw flour taste.
7. Slowly pour in the beef broth and Worcestershire sauce, stirring constantly to prevent lumps from forming. Bring the mixture to a simmer and cook until the gravy thickens, about 5-7 minutes.
8. Season the gravy with salt and pepper to taste.
9. Return the cooked beef patties to the skillet, spooning some of the mushroom gravy over the top.
10. Simmer the Salisbury steaks in the gravy for another 5-10 minutes, until heated through and the flavors meld together.
11. Garnish with chopped fresh parsley, if desired, before serving.

Serve the Salisbury steak hot, accompanied by mashed potatoes, rice, or noodles, and your favorite vegetable side dish. Enjoy this comforting and flavorful American classic!

Shrimp Scampi

Ingredients:

- 1 pound large shrimp, peeled and deveined
- Salt and pepper, to taste
- 3 tablespoons unsalted butter
- 2 tablespoons olive oil
- 4 cloves garlic, minced
- 1/4 teaspoon red pepper flakes (optional)
- 1/4 cup white wine
- 2 tablespoons fresh lemon juice
- Zest of 1 lemon
- 1/4 cup chopped fresh parsley
- Cooked pasta, for serving (such as spaghetti or linguine)
- Lemon wedges, for serving
- Additional chopped parsley, for garnish (optional)

Instructions:

1. Pat the shrimp dry with paper towels and season with salt and pepper to taste.
2. In a large skillet, heat the butter and olive oil over medium-high heat until the butter is melted and foamy.
3. Add the minced garlic and red pepper flakes (if using) to the skillet, and sauté for about 1 minute, or until the garlic is fragrant.
4. Add the seasoned shrimp to the skillet in a single layer. Cook for 1-2 minutes on each side, until the shrimp turn pink and opaque. Be careful not to overcook the shrimp.
5. Remove the cooked shrimp from the skillet and transfer them to a plate. Cover to keep warm.
6. Deglaze the skillet with white wine, scraping up any browned bits from the bottom of the pan. Let the wine simmer for 1-2 minutes to reduce slightly.
7. Stir in the fresh lemon juice and lemon zest, and return the cooked shrimp to the skillet. Toss to coat the shrimp in the sauce.
8. Remove the skillet from heat and stir in the chopped fresh parsley.
9. Serve the Shrimp Scampi hot over cooked pasta, garnished with additional chopped parsley if desired, and lemon wedges on the side.

10. Enjoy this flavorful and aromatic dish with crusty bread for soaking up the delicious sauce.

Shrimp Scampi is quick and easy to make, yet it's elegant enough to serve for a special dinner or celebration. Enjoy the vibrant flavors of garlic, lemon, and herbs in every bite!

Sole Meunière

Ingredients:

- 4 sole fillets (about 6-8 ounces each), skin removed
- Salt and pepper, to taste
- 1/2 cup all-purpose flour, for dredging
- 4 tablespoons unsalted butter
- 2 tablespoons olive oil
- 2 tablespoons fresh lemon juice
- 2 tablespoons chopped fresh parsley
- Lemon wedges, for serving

Instructions:

1. Pat the sole fillets dry with paper towels and season them with salt and pepper on both sides.
2. Dredge the seasoned sole fillets in the flour, shaking off any excess.
3. In a large skillet, heat 2 tablespoons of butter and 1 tablespoon of olive oil over medium-high heat until the butter is melted and foamy.
4. Carefully add the dredged sole fillets to the skillet in a single layer. Cook for about 2-3 minutes on each side, or until golden brown and cooked through. Be careful not to overcrowd the skillet; you may need to cook the fillets in batches.
5. Once the sole fillets are cooked, transfer them to a serving platter or individual plates. Cover with foil to keep warm.
6. In the same skillet, add the remaining 2 tablespoons of butter and 1 tablespoon of olive oil. Cook over medium heat until the butter is melted and starts to brown slightly, about 2-3 minutes.
7. Remove the skillet from heat and carefully add the fresh lemon juice to the browned butter, swirling the skillet to combine.
8. Pour the lemon butter sauce over the cooked sole fillets.
9. Sprinkle the chopped fresh parsley over the top of the sole fillets.
10. Serve the Sole Meunière hot, accompanied by lemon wedges on the side.
11. Enjoy this elegant and flavorful dish with a side of steamed vegetables or a simple green salad.

Sole Meunière is a classic French dish that showcases the delicate flavor of sole fish with a simple yet exquisite sauce. It's perfect for a special dinner or any occasion when you want to impress with a delicious and refined dish!

Steak Diane

Ingredients:

- 4 beef tenderloin steaks (about 6-8 ounces each), 1 inch thick
- Salt and pepper, to taste
- 2 tablespoons unsalted butter
- 1 tablespoon olive oil
- 2 shallots, finely chopped
- 8 ounces cremini or button mushrooms, sliced
- 2 cloves garlic, minced
- 1/4 cup brandy or Cognac
- 1/2 cup beef broth
- 2 tablespoons Dijon mustard
- 1/4 cup heavy cream
- 2 tablespoons chopped fresh parsley, for garnish

Instructions:

1. Pat the steaks dry with paper towels and season them generously with salt and pepper on both sides.
2. In a large skillet, heat 1 tablespoon of butter and the olive oil over medium-high heat until the butter is melted and hot.
3. Add the seasoned steaks to the skillet and cook for about 3-4 minutes on each side for medium-rare, or until cooked to your desired doneness. Transfer the cooked steaks to a plate and cover loosely with foil to keep warm.
4. In the same skillet, add the remaining tablespoon of butter. Once melted, add the chopped shallots and sliced mushrooms to the skillet. Cook, stirring occasionally, until the mushrooms are golden brown and the shallots are softened, about 5-7 minutes.
5. Add the minced garlic to the skillet and cook for an additional minute, until fragrant.
6. Carefully pour the brandy or Cognac into the skillet, stirring to deglaze the pan and scrape up any browned bits from the bottom. Let the alcohol cook off for about 1-2 minutes.
7. Stir in the beef broth and Dijon mustard, and bring the mixture to a simmer. Let it cook for 2-3 minutes to reduce slightly.
8. Reduce the heat to low and stir in the heavy cream. Simmer gently for another 2-3 minutes, until the sauce thickens slightly.

9. Return the cooked steaks to the skillet, turning them in the sauce to coat evenly. Let them warm through for a minute or two.
10. Remove the skillet from heat and garnish the Steak Diane with chopped fresh parsley.
11. Serve the Steak Diane hot, accompanied by your favorite side dishes, such as mashed potatoes, steamed vegetables, or a crisp green salad.

Enjoy this indulgent and flavorful dish with its rich and creamy pan sauce, perfect for a special dinner or celebration!

Tournedos Rossini

Ingredients:

- 4 beef tenderloin steaks (about 6-8 ounces each), 1 1/2 inches thick
- Salt and pepper, to taste
- 4 slices brioche or crusty French bread, toasted
- 4 slices foie gras (about 2 ounces each)
- 2 tablespoons unsalted butter
- 2 tablespoons olive oil
- 1/4 cup Madeira wine
- 1/2 cup beef broth
- 1 tablespoon demi-glace or beef demi-glace concentrate
- Chopped fresh parsley, for garnish (optional)
- Truffle slices or truffle oil, for garnish (optional)

Instructions:

1. Pat the beef tenderloin steaks dry with paper towels and season them generously with salt and pepper on both sides.
2. In a large skillet, heat the butter and olive oil over medium-high heat until the butter is melted and hot.
3. Add the seasoned beef tenderloin steaks to the skillet and cook for about 3-4 minutes on each side for medium-rare, or until cooked to your desired doneness. Transfer the cooked steaks to a plate and cover loosely with foil to keep warm.
4. In the same skillet, add the slices of foie gras. Sear for about 1-2 minutes on each side, until golden brown and caramelized. Transfer the seared foie gras to the plate with the cooked steaks.
5. Deglaze the skillet with Madeira wine, scraping up any browned bits from the bottom of the pan. Let the wine cook down for about 1-2 minutes.
6. Stir in the beef broth and demi-glace, and bring the sauce to a simmer. Let it cook for 3-4 minutes, until slightly thickened.
7. Return the cooked beef tenderloin steaks and seared foie gras to the skillet, turning them in the sauce to coat evenly. Let them warm through for a minute or two.
8. Place a slice of toasted brioche or French bread on each serving plate. Top each slice of bread with a beef tenderloin steak, followed by a slice of seared foie gras.
9. Spoon the Madeira sauce over the top of each tournedos Rossini.

10. Garnish the tournedos Rossini with chopped fresh parsley and truffle slices or a drizzle of truffle oil, if desired.
11. Serve the tournedos Rossini hot, accompanied by your favorite side dishes, such as roasted potatoes or sautéed vegetables.

Enjoy this decadent and elegant dish, perfect for a special occasion or a gourmet dinner experience!

Waldorf Salad

Ingredients:

- 2 large crisp apples (such as Granny Smith or Honeycrisp), cored and diced
- 1 cup celery, thinly sliced
- 1 cup red seedless grapes, halved
- 1/2 cup walnuts, chopped
- 1/2 cup mayonnaise
- 2 tablespoons lemon juice
- 1 tablespoon honey (optional)
- Salt and pepper, to taste
- Lettuce leaves, for serving (optional)

Instructions:

1. In a large mixing bowl, combine the diced apples, sliced celery, halved grapes, and chopped walnuts.
2. In a small bowl, whisk together the mayonnaise, lemon juice, and honey (if using) until well combined. Season with salt and pepper to taste.
3. Pour the dressing over the apple mixture in the large bowl, and toss gently until everything is evenly coated.
4. Cover the bowl with plastic wrap and refrigerate the Waldorf Salad for at least 30 minutes to allow the flavors to meld together.
5. Just before serving, give the salad a final toss to redistribute the dressing.
6. If desired, serve the Waldorf Salad on a bed of lettuce leaves for a beautiful presentation.
7. Enjoy the Waldorf Salad as a refreshing side dish or light lunch option.

Feel free to customize the Waldorf Salad to your taste preferences by adding ingredients like raisins, dried cranberries, or even chicken for a heartier version. It's a versatile and timeless dish that's perfect for any occasion!

Welsh Rarebit

Ingredients:

- 2 tablespoons unsalted butter
- 2 tablespoons all-purpose flour
- 1 cup beer (traditional choices include ale or stout)
- 1 teaspoon Worcestershire sauce
- 1 teaspoon Dijon mustard
- 1/2 teaspoon smoked paprika (optional)
- 2 cups shredded sharp Cheddar cheese
- Salt and pepper, to taste
- 4 slices bread, toasted
- Chopped fresh parsley, for garnish (optional)

Instructions:

1. In a medium saucepan, melt the butter over medium heat.
2. Once the butter is melted, add the flour to the saucepan and whisk continuously for 1-2 minutes to create a roux. Cook until the roux turns a light golden color.
3. Gradually pour in the beer while whisking constantly to prevent lumps from forming. Continue to whisk until the mixture is smooth.
4. Stir in the Worcestershire sauce, Dijon mustard, and smoked paprika (if using). Cook the mixture for another 2-3 minutes, stirring occasionally.
5. Reduce the heat to low and gradually add the shredded Cheddar cheese to the saucepan, stirring until the cheese is completely melted and the sauce is smooth.
6. Season the cheese sauce with salt and pepper to taste. Keep warm over low heat while you prepare the toast.
7. Toast the slices of bread until golden brown and crisp.
8. Place the toasted bread slices on serving plates.
9. Spoon the warm cheese sauce generously over the toast.
10. Garnish the Welsh Rarebit with chopped fresh parsley, if desired.
11. Serve the Welsh Rarebit immediately, while the cheese sauce is still warm and gooey.

Enjoy this comforting and flavorful dish as a satisfying snack, appetizer, or light meal!

Beef Burgundy

Ingredients:

- 2 pounds beef chuck, cut into 1-inch cubes
- Salt and pepper, to taste
- 2 tablespoons all-purpose flour
- 2 tablespoons olive oil
- 4 slices bacon, diced
- 1 onion, chopped
- 2 carrots, sliced
- 2 cloves garlic, minced
- 2 cups red wine (such as Burgundy or Pinot Noir)
- 1 cup beef broth
- 2 tablespoons tomato paste
- 1 tablespoon Dijon mustard
- 1 teaspoon dried thyme
- 2 bay leaves
- 8 ounces mushrooms, quartered
- Chopped fresh parsley, for garnish (optional)

Instructions:

1. Preheat your oven to 325°F (165°C).
2. Season the beef cubes generously with salt and pepper, then dredge them in the flour, shaking off any excess.
3. Heat the olive oil in a large Dutch oven or oven-safe pot over medium-high heat. Add the beef cubes in batches and cook until browned on all sides. Remove the browned beef cubes from the pot and set aside.
4. In the same pot, add the diced bacon and cook until browned and crispy. Remove the bacon from the pot and set aside with the beef.
5. Add the chopped onion and sliced carrots to the pot, and cook until softened, about 5 minutes. Add the minced garlic and cook for an additional minute.
6. Return the browned beef and bacon to the pot. Pour in the red wine and beef broth, stirring to scrape up any browned bits from the bottom of the pot.
7. Stir in the tomato paste, Dijon mustard, dried thyme, and bay leaves. Bring the mixture to a simmer.
8. Cover the pot with a lid and transfer it to the preheated oven. Cook for 2-3 hours, or until the beef is tender and the sauce has thickened.

9. About 30 minutes before the Beef Burgundy is done, add the quartered mushrooms to the pot and stir to combine.
10. Once the beef is tender and the sauce has thickened to your liking, remove the pot from the oven.
11. Discard the bay leaves and adjust seasoning with salt and pepper, if needed.
12. Serve the Beef Burgundy hot, garnished with chopped fresh parsley, if desired.

Beef Burgundy pairs wonderfully with mashed potatoes, egg noodles, or crusty bread for soaking up the delicious sauce. Enjoy this comforting and flavorful French stew!

Bouillabaisse

Ingredients:

- 2 tablespoons olive oil
- 1 onion, chopped
- 2 cloves garlic, minced
- 1 fennel bulb, sliced
- 1 leek, sliced
- 1 celery stalk, sliced
- 1 carrot, sliced
- 1/2 teaspoon saffron threads
- 1 bay leaf
- 1 sprig fresh thyme
- 1 sprig fresh parsley
- 1 can (14 oz) diced tomatoes, with juices
- 4 cups fish stock or seafood broth
- 1 cup dry white wine
- Salt and pepper, to taste
- 1 pound mixed fish fillets (such as cod, halibut, snapper), cut into chunks
- 1/2 pound shellfish (such as shrimp, mussels, clams)
- Crusty bread, for serving
- Rouille sauce (optional, for serving)

Instructions:

1. Heat the olive oil in a large Dutch oven or stockpot over medium heat. Add the chopped onion and minced garlic, and cook until softened and fragrant, about 5 minutes.
2. Add the sliced fennel, leek, celery, and carrot to the pot, and cook for another 5 minutes, until the vegetables start to soften.
3. Stir in the saffron threads, bay leaf, fresh thyme, and parsley sprigs. Cook for another minute to toast the saffron.
4. Add the diced tomatoes (with their juices), fish stock, and white wine to the pot. Season with salt and pepper to taste. Bring the mixture to a simmer and let it cook for about 20 minutes to allow the flavors to meld together.
5. Once the broth has simmered and the vegetables are tender, add the mixed fish fillets and shellfish to the pot. Cover and simmer gently for about 5-7 minutes, or

until the fish is cooked through and the shellfish have opened (discard any unopened shells).
6. Taste and adjust seasoning with additional salt and pepper, if needed.
7. Ladle the Bouillabaisse into serving bowls, making sure to distribute the fish, shellfish, and vegetables evenly.
8. Serve the Bouillabaisse hot, accompanied by crusty bread for dipping. You can also serve Rouille sauce on the side for extra flavor.

Bouillabaisse is a hearty and comforting dish that's perfect for showcasing the fresh flavors of the sea. Enjoy this iconic French stew as a main course for a special occasion or festive meal!

Chicken Marengo

Ingredients:

- 4 bone-in, skin-on chicken thighs
- Salt and pepper, to taste
- 2 tablespoons olive oil
- 1 onion, finely chopped
- 2 cloves garlic, minced
- 8 ounces mushrooms, sliced
- 1 can (14 oz) diced tomatoes, with juices
- 1/2 cup dry white wine
- 1/2 cup chicken broth
- 1 teaspoon dried thyme
- 1 bay leaf
- 2 tablespoons chopped fresh parsley, for garnish
- Cooked rice or crusty bread, for serving

Instructions:

1. Season the chicken thighs generously with salt and pepper.
2. Heat the olive oil in a large skillet or Dutch oven over medium-high heat. Add the chicken thighs to the skillet, skin-side down, and cook until golden brown and crispy, about 5 minutes per side. Remove the chicken from the skillet and set aside.
3. In the same skillet, add the chopped onion and minced garlic. Cook, stirring occasionally, until the onion is softened and translucent, about 3-4 minutes.
4. Add the sliced mushrooms to the skillet and cook until they release their moisture and start to brown, about 5 minutes.
5. Stir in the diced tomatoes (with their juices), dry white wine, chicken broth, dried thyme, and bay leaf. Bring the mixture to a simmer.
6. Return the browned chicken thighs to the skillet, nestling them into the sauce. Cover the skillet with a lid and let the chicken simmer gently in the sauce for about 20-25 minutes, or until the chicken is cooked through and tender.
7. Once the chicken is cooked, remove the skillet from heat and discard the bay leaf. Taste the sauce and adjust seasoning with salt and pepper, if needed.
8. Garnish the Chicken Marengo with chopped fresh parsley.
9. Serve the Chicken Marengo hot, spooned over cooked rice or accompanied by crusty bread for soaking up the delicious sauce.

Chicken Marengo is a comforting and flavorful dish with a rich history. Enjoy this French classic as a hearty meal for dinner or a special occasion!

Chicken Cordon Bleu

Ingredients:

- 4 boneless, skinless chicken breasts
- Salt and pepper, to taste
- 4 slices Swiss cheese
- 4 slices ham
- 1/2 cup all-purpose flour
- 2 large eggs
- 1 cup breadcrumbs (plain or seasoned)
- 2 tablespoons olive oil or melted butter

Instructions:

1. Preheat your oven to 375°F (190°C).
2. Place each chicken breast between two sheets of plastic wrap or parchment paper. Use a meat mallet or rolling pin to pound the chicken breasts to an even thickness of about 1/4 inch. Season both sides of the chicken breasts with salt and pepper.
3. Place a slice of Swiss cheese and a slice of ham on each chicken breast.
4. Roll up each chicken breast tightly, enclosing the cheese and ham inside, and secure the seam with toothpicks.
5. Set up a breading station with three shallow bowls: one with flour, one with beaten eggs, and one with breadcrumbs.
6. Dredge each chicken roll-up in the flour, shaking off any excess. Dip it into the beaten eggs, then coat it evenly with breadcrumbs, pressing gently to adhere.
7. Place the breaded chicken roll-ups on a baking sheet lined with parchment paper.
8. Drizzle the olive oil or melted butter over the chicken roll-ups.
9. Bake in the preheated oven for 25-30 minutes, or until the chicken is cooked through and the breadcrumbs are golden and crispy.
10. Remove the chicken Cordon Bleu from the oven and let them rest for a few minutes before serving.
11. Carefully remove the toothpicks from the chicken roll-ups before serving.
12. Serve the Chicken Cordon Bleu hot, accompanied by your favorite side dishes, such as mashed potatoes, steamed vegetables, or a fresh green salad.

Enjoy this classic and comforting dish with its delicious combination of tender chicken, savory ham, and melted cheese!

Coquilles St. Jacques

Ingredients:

- 1 pound fresh scallops, cleaned and patted dry
- Salt and pepper, to taste
- 2 tablespoons unsalted butter
- 1 shallot, finely chopped
- 2 cloves garlic, minced
- 8 ounces mushrooms, sliced
- 1/2 cup dry white wine
- 1 cup heavy cream
- 1 tablespoon all-purpose flour
- 1/4 cup grated Gruyère cheese
- 1/4 cup breadcrumbs
- Chopped fresh parsley, for garnish

Instructions:

1. Preheat your oven to 400°F (200°C).
2. Season the scallops with salt and pepper to taste.
3. In a large skillet, melt 1 tablespoon of butter over medium-high heat. Add the scallops to the skillet and cook for about 1-2 minutes per side, until lightly browned and cooked through. Remove the scallops from the skillet and set aside.
4. In the same skillet, melt the remaining tablespoon of butter. Add the chopped shallot and minced garlic, and cook until softened and fragrant, about 2 minutes.
5. Add the sliced mushrooms to the skillet and cook until they release their moisture and start to brown, about 5 minutes.
6. Pour in the white wine and simmer for a few minutes to reduce slightly.
7. In a small bowl, whisk together the heavy cream and flour until smooth. Pour the cream mixture into the skillet, stirring to combine. Cook for another 2-3 minutes, until the sauce thickens.
8. Return the cooked scallops to the skillet, tossing them in the sauce to coat evenly.
9. Divide the scallops and sauce among scallop shells or individual oven-safe dishes.
10. In a small bowl, mix together the grated Gruyère cheese and breadcrumbs. Sprinkle the breadcrumb mixture over the top of each scallop dish.

11. Place the scallop dishes on a baking sheet and bake in the preheated oven for 10-12 minutes, or until the breadcrumbs are golden brown and crispy.
12. Remove the Coquilles St. Jacques from the oven and garnish with chopped fresh parsley before serving.

Enjoy this elegant and indulgent dish as an appetizer or main course, accompanied by crusty bread or a side salad. It's perfect for special occasions or a fancy dinner at home!

Crêpes Suzette

Ingredients:

For the Crêpes:

- 1 cup all-purpose flour
- 2 large eggs
- 1 cup milk
- 2 tablespoons unsalted butter, melted
- 1 tablespoon granulated sugar
- Pinch of salt
- Butter or oil, for cooking the crêpes

For the Suzette Sauce:

- 1/2 cup unsalted butter
- 1/2 cup granulated sugar
- Zest of 1 orange
- 1/2 cup fresh orange juice (from about 2 oranges)
- 1/4 cup Grand Marnier or Cointreau (optional)

Instructions:

1. To make the crêpe batter, whisk together the flour, eggs, milk, melted butter, sugar, and salt in a large mixing bowl until smooth. Let the batter rest for at least 30 minutes at room temperature.
2. Heat a non-stick skillet or crêpe pan over medium heat. Brush the skillet with a little butter or oil.
3. Pour a small ladleful of batter into the skillet, swirling it around to coat the bottom evenly. Cook the crêpe for about 1-2 minutes, or until lightly golden on the bottom. Flip the crêpe and cook for another 1-2 minutes on the other side. Repeat with the remaining batter, stacking the cooked crêpes on a plate.
4. To make the Suzette sauce, melt the butter in a skillet over medium heat. Stir in the granulated sugar and orange zest, and cook until the sugar is dissolved and the mixture is bubbling and golden brown.

5. Carefully pour in the orange juice and Grand Marnier or Cointreau (if using), stirring to combine. Let the sauce simmer for a few minutes until slightly thickened.
6. Fold each crêpe into quarters and place them in the skillet with the Suzette sauce. Gently heat the crêpes in the sauce for a minute or two, turning them once to coat evenly.
7. To serve, transfer the crêpes to individual plates and spoon some of the Suzette sauce over the top.
8. Optionally, you can flambé the Crêpes Suzette by carefully igniting the sauce with a long match or lighter.
9. Garnish the Crêpes Suzette with additional orange zest or segments, if desired.
10. Serve the Crêpes Suzette immediately while they are still warm and enjoy the rich, citrusy flavors!

Crêpes Suzette is a delightful and elegant dessert that's perfect for special occasions or a fancy dinner party. Enjoy the theatrical presentation and indulgent taste of this classic French treat!

Duck à l'Orange

Ingredients:

For the Duck:

- 2 duck breasts, skin-on
- Salt and pepper, to taste

For the Orange Sauce:

- 2 oranges
- 1/2 cup orange juice
- 1/4 cup sugar
- 1/4 cup white wine vinegar
- 1/4 cup chicken broth
- 2 tablespoons Grand Marnier or Cointreau (optional)
- Salt and pepper, to taste

Instructions:

1. Preheat your oven to 400°F (200°C).
2. Score the skin of the duck breasts in a crosshatch pattern, being careful not to cut into the meat. Season both sides of the duck breasts with salt and pepper.
3. Heat a skillet over medium-high heat. Place the duck breasts in the skillet, skin-side down, and cook for about 6-8 minutes, until the skin is golden and crispy. Flip the duck breasts and cook for another 2-3 minutes on the other side. Transfer the duck breasts to a baking dish, skin-side up.
4. Roast the duck breasts in the preheated oven for about 10-12 minutes for medium-rare or until cooked to your desired doneness. Remove the duck breasts from the oven and let them rest for a few minutes before slicing.
5. While the duck is roasting, prepare the orange sauce. Zest one of the oranges and set the zest aside. Juice both oranges.
6. In a saucepan, combine the orange juice, sugar, white wine vinegar, chicken broth, and orange zest. Bring the mixture to a boil over medium-high heat, then reduce the heat to medium-low and let it simmer for about 15-20 minutes, or until the sauce is slightly thickened and syrupy.

7. Stir in the Grand Marnier or Cointreau (if using), and season the sauce with salt and pepper to taste.
8. Once the duck breasts are rested, slice them thinly on the diagonal.
9. To serve, arrange the sliced duck breasts on serving plates and drizzle the orange sauce over the top.
10. Garnish the Duck à l'Orange with additional orange zest, if desired.
11. Serve the Duck à l'Orange hot, accompanied by your favorite side dishes, such as roasted potatoes, steamed vegetables, or a fresh green salad.

Enjoy this elegant and flavorful French dish with its perfect balance of rich duck and bright orange flavors!

Eggs à la Goldenrod

Ingredients:

- 6 large eggs
- 2 tablespoons unsalted butter
- 2 tablespoons all-purpose flour
- 1 cup milk
- Salt and pepper, to taste
- 4 slices bread, toasted
- Chopped fresh parsley or chives, for garnish (optional)
- Paprika, for garnish (optional)

Instructions:

1. Hard-boil the eggs: Place the eggs in a saucepan and cover them with cold water. Bring the water to a boil over medium-high heat. Once boiling, cover the saucepan and remove it from heat. Let the eggs sit in the hot water for 10-12 minutes. Then, drain the hot water and transfer the eggs to a bowl of ice water to cool completely. Once cooled, peel the eggs and separate the whites from the yolks.
2. Make the white sauce: In a saucepan, melt the butter over medium heat. Stir in the flour and cook, stirring constantly, for about 1 minute to make a roux. Gradually whisk in the milk, stirring constantly to prevent lumps from forming. Cook the sauce until thickened, about 3-4 minutes. Season with salt and pepper to taste.
3. Assemble the dish: Chop the egg whites and set aside. Add the chopped egg yolks to the white sauce, reserving a small amount for garnish if desired. Stir to combine.
4. Place the toasted bread slices on serving plates. Spoon the creamy egg sauce over the toast.
5. Sprinkle the chopped egg whites over the top of the sauce.
6. Garnish with chopped fresh parsley or chives, and a sprinkle of paprika, if desired.
7. Serve the Eggs à la Goldenrod hot, as a comforting and satisfying breakfast or brunch dish.

Enjoy this classic and comforting dish with its creamy sauce and hearty eggs served over crispy toast!

Lobster Thermidor

Ingredients:

- 2 cooked lobsters (about 1 1/2 pounds each)
- 4 tablespoons unsalted butter
- 1 shallot, finely chopped
- 2 cloves garlic, minced
- 1/4 cup all-purpose flour
- 1 cup whole milk
- 1/4 cup heavy cream
- 1/4 cup grated Gruyère cheese
- 2 tablespoons grated Parmesan cheese
- 2 tablespoons chopped fresh parsley
- 2 tablespoons chopped fresh tarragon (or 1 teaspoon dried tarragon)
- 2 tablespoons brandy or Cognac
- Salt and pepper, to taste
- Lemon wedges, for serving

Instructions:

1. Preheat your oven's broiler.
2. Use kitchen shears or a sharp knife to split the lobsters in half lengthwise. Remove the meat from the shells, keeping the shells intact, and chop the meat into bite-sized pieces. Reserve the shells.
3. In a large skillet, melt the butter over medium heat. Add the chopped shallot and minced garlic, and sauté until softened and fragrant, about 2 minutes.
4. Sprinkle the flour over the butter mixture and stir to combine. Cook, stirring constantly, for about 2 minutes to cook out the raw flour taste.
5. Gradually whisk in the milk and heavy cream, stirring constantly to prevent lumps from forming. Cook the sauce until thickened, about 5 minutes.
6. Stir in the grated Gruyère cheese, grated Parmesan cheese, chopped parsley, chopped tarragon, and brandy or Cognac. Season the sauce with salt and pepper to taste.
7. Add the chopped lobster meat to the sauce, stirring to coat evenly.
8. Arrange the reserved lobster shells on a baking sheet or in a baking dish. Spoon the lobster mixture back into the shells, dividing it evenly among them.
9. Sprinkle additional grated Gruyère cheese over the top of each lobster shell.

10. Place the lobster shells under the preheated broiler and broil for 4-5 minutes, or until the cheese is melted and golden brown.
11. Remove the Lobster Thermidor from the oven and garnish with additional chopped parsley, if desired.
12. Serve the Lobster Thermidor hot, accompanied by lemon wedges for squeezing over the top.

Enjoy this elegant and indulgent dish as a special treat for a festive dinner or celebration!

Oysters Bienville

Ingredients:

- 12 fresh oysters, shucked, with their juices
- 4 tablespoons unsalted butter
- 1/4 cup all-purpose flour
- 1 cup milk
- 1/2 cup heavy cream
- 1/4 cup dry white wine
- 1/4 cup grated Parmesan cheese
- 2 tablespoons chopped green onions
- 2 tablespoons chopped fresh parsley
- 1 tablespoon chopped fresh thyme (or 1 teaspoon dried thyme)
- 1/4 teaspoon cayenne pepper (optional)
- Salt and pepper, to taste
- 1/2 cup breadcrumbs
- Lemon wedges, for serving

Instructions:

1. Preheat your oven to 400°F (200°C).
2. In a saucepan, melt the butter over medium heat. Stir in the flour to form a roux. Cook the roux, stirring constantly, for about 2 minutes to cook out the raw flour taste.
3. Gradually whisk in the milk, heavy cream, and dry white wine, stirring constantly to prevent lumps from forming. Cook the sauce until thickened, about 5 minutes.
4. Stir in the grated Parmesan cheese, chopped green onions, chopped parsley, chopped thyme, and cayenne pepper (if using). Season the sauce with salt and pepper to taste.
5. Add the shucked oysters and their juices to the saucepan, stirring gently to coat the oysters in the sauce. Cook for 2-3 minutes, until the edges of the oysters start to curl.
6. Divide the oyster mixture evenly among individual ovenproof dishes or a baking dish.
7. Sprinkle the breadcrumbs evenly over the top of the oyster mixture.
8. Place the dishes or baking dish in the preheated oven and bake for about 10-12 minutes, or until the breadcrumbs are golden brown and the sauce is bubbly.

9. Remove the Oysters Bienville from the oven and let them cool slightly before serving.
10. Serve the Oysters Bienville hot, accompanied by lemon wedges for squeezing over the top.

Enjoy this decadent and flavorful New Orleans specialty as an appetizer or main course for a special occasion or festive gathering!

Peach Melba

Ingredients:

For the Poached Peaches:

- 4 ripe peaches
- 1 cup water
- 1/2 cup granulated sugar
- 1 teaspoon vanilla extract

For the Raspberry Sauce:

- 1 cup fresh or frozen raspberries
- 2 tablespoons granulated sugar
- 1 tablespoon lemon juice

For Serving:

- Vanilla ice cream
- Fresh raspberries, for garnish (optional)
- Mint leaves, for garnish (optional)

Instructions:

1. Prepare the poached peaches: Bring a large pot of water to a boil. Using a sharp knife, score a small "X" on the bottom of each peach. Carefully lower the peaches into the boiling water and blanch them for about 30 seconds. Remove the peaches with a slotted spoon and immediately transfer them to a bowl of ice water to stop the cooking process.
2. Once the peaches are cool enough to handle, peel off the skins. Cut each peach in half and remove the pits.
3. In a saucepan, combine the water, sugar, and vanilla extract. Bring the mixture to a simmer over medium heat, stirring until the sugar is dissolved.
4. Add the peach halves to the simmering syrup. Reduce the heat to low and poach the peaches for about 5-7 minutes, or until they are tender but still hold their shape. Remove the peaches from the syrup using a slotted spoon and let them cool slightly.
5. Prepare the raspberry sauce: In a blender or food processor, puree the raspberries, sugar, and lemon juice until smooth. Strain the mixture through a

fine-mesh sieve to remove the seeds. Discard the seeds and refrigerate the sauce until ready to use.
6. To serve, place a scoop of vanilla ice cream in each serving dish. Arrange a few poached peach halves around the ice cream.
7. Drizzle the raspberry sauce over the peaches and ice cream.
8. Garnish the Peach Melba with fresh raspberries and mint leaves, if desired.
9. Serve the Peach Melba immediately, while the ice cream is still cold and the peaches are warm.

Enjoy this elegant and refreshing dessert that's perfect for showcasing ripe summer peaches and bright raspberry flavor!

Pheasant à la Kiev

Ingredients:

For the Herb Butter:

- 1/2 cup unsalted butter, softened
- 2 tablespoons chopped fresh parsley
- 1 tablespoon chopped fresh dill
- 1 tablespoon chopped fresh chives
- 2 cloves garlic, minced
- 1 teaspoon lemon juice
- Salt and pepper, to taste

For the Pheasant:

- 4 pheasant breasts, boneless and skinless
- Salt and pepper, to taste
- 1/2 cup all-purpose flour
- 2 large eggs, beaten
- 1 cup breadcrumbs (plain or seasoned)
- Vegetable oil, for frying
- Lemon wedges, for serving

Instructions:

1. Prepare the herb butter: In a small bowl, combine the softened butter, chopped parsley, chopped dill, chopped chives, minced garlic, lemon juice, salt, and pepper. Mix until well combined. Place the herb butter mixture on a piece of plastic wrap or parchment paper, shape it into a log, and refrigerate until firm.
2. Butterfly the pheasant breasts: Place each pheasant breast between two sheets of plastic wrap or parchment paper. Use a meat mallet or rolling pin to gently pound the breasts to an even thickness of about 1/4 inch. Season both sides of the pheasant breasts with salt and pepper.
3. Remove the herb butter from the refrigerator and slice it into 4 equal portions.
4. Place a portion of herb butter in the center of each flattened pheasant breast. Fold the sides of the breast over the butter to enclose it completely, then roll it up tightly. Secure the ends with toothpicks to hold the shape. Repeat with the remaining pheasant breasts and herb butter portions.

5. Set up a breading station: Place the flour, beaten eggs, and breadcrumbs in three separate shallow bowls.
6. Dredge each stuffed pheasant breast in the flour, shaking off any excess. Dip it into the beaten eggs, then coat it evenly with breadcrumbs, pressing gently to adhere. Repeat with the remaining stuffed pheasant breasts.
7. Heat vegetable oil in a large skillet over medium-high heat. Fry the breaded pheasant breasts in the hot oil until golden brown and crispy on all sides, about 5-6 minutes per side.
8. Transfer the fried Pheasant à la Kiev to a paper towel-lined plate to drain excess oil.
9. Remove the toothpicks from the Pheasant à la Kiev before serving.
10. Serve the Pheasant à la Kiev hot, accompanied by lemon wedges for squeezing over the top.

Enjoy this elegant and flavorful dish that's sure to impress your guests with its tender pheasant and herby buttery filling!

Potage Parmentier (Potato Leek Soup)

Ingredients:

- 2 tablespoons unsalted butter
- 2 leeks, white and light green parts only, sliced
- 1 onion, chopped
- 2 garlic cloves, minced
- 4 large potatoes, peeled and diced
- 4 cups chicken or vegetable broth
- 1 bay leaf
- Salt and pepper, to taste
- 1/2 cup heavy cream (optional)
- Chopped chives or parsley, for garnish (optional)

Instructions:

1. In a large pot or Dutch oven, melt the butter over medium heat. Add the sliced leeks and chopped onion, and cook until softened, about 5 minutes.
2. Add the minced garlic to the pot and cook for an additional minute, until fragrant.
3. Add the diced potatoes to the pot, along with the chicken or vegetable broth and bay leaf. Season with salt and pepper to taste.
4. Bring the soup to a boil, then reduce the heat to low and simmer, partially covered, for about 20-25 minutes, or until the potatoes are tender and can be easily pierced with a fork.
5. Remove the bay leaf from the soup and discard it.
6. Using an immersion blender or regular blender, puree the soup until smooth. Be careful when blending hot liquids.
7. If using, stir in the heavy cream to the soup until well combined. Adjust seasoning with salt and pepper, if needed.
8. Ladle the Potato Leek Soup into bowls and garnish with chopped chives or parsley, if desired.
9. Serve the soup hot, accompanied by crusty bread or a side salad, if desired.

Enjoy this comforting and creamy Potato Leek Soup, perfect for a cozy meal on a chilly day!

Quenelles de Brochet

Ingredients:

For the Quenelles:

- 1 pound pike fish fillets, skinned and deboned
- 2 eggs
- 1/2 cup heavy cream
- 1/2 cup breadcrumbs
- Salt and white pepper, to taste
- Pinch of nutmeg
- Butter, for greasing

For the Sauce:

- 2 cups fish or chicken broth
- 2 tablespoons unsalted butter
- 2 tablespoons all-purpose flour
- 1/2 cup heavy cream
- Salt and white pepper, to taste
- Lemon juice, to taste
- Chopped fresh parsley, for garnish

Instructions:

1. Prepare the Quenelles: In a food processor, blend the pike fish fillets until smooth. Add the eggs, heavy cream, breadcrumbs, salt, white pepper, and nutmeg. Process until well combined and the mixture is smooth.
2. Transfer the fish mixture to a bowl, cover, and refrigerate for at least 30 minutes to firm up.
3. Meanwhile, prepare the Sauce: In a saucepan, heat the fish or chicken broth over medium heat until simmering.
4. In another saucepan, melt the butter over medium heat. Stir in the flour to form a roux and cook, stirring constantly, for 2-3 minutes until golden brown.
5. Gradually whisk in the hot broth, stirring constantly to prevent lumps from forming. Cook the sauce until thickened, about 5 minutes.
6. Stir in the heavy cream and season with salt, white pepper, and lemon juice to taste. Keep the sauce warm over low heat while you prepare the quenelles.

7. Preheat your oven to 350°F (175°C). Butter a baking dish or casserole dish.
8. Shape the chilled fish mixture into oval-shaped quenelles using two spoons or wet hands. Place the quenelles in the prepared baking dish, leaving a little space between each one.
9. Fill a large skillet or saucepan with water and bring it to a gentle simmer over medium heat. Carefully lower the quenelles into the simmering water and poach them for about 5 minutes, or until they are cooked through and firm.
10. Using a slotted spoon, transfer the poached quenelles to the prepared baking dish.
11. Pour the warm sauce over the quenelles in the baking dish, covering them completely.
12. Bake the Quenelles de Brochet in the preheated oven for 15-20 minutes, or until the sauce is bubbling and the quenelles are lightly browned on top.
13. Garnish the Quenelles de Brochet with chopped fresh parsley before serving.

Enjoy this elegant and delicious French dish as a main course for a special dinner or celebration!

Rabbit Stew

Ingredients:

- 1 whole rabbit, cleaned and cut into pieces
- 2 tablespoons olive oil or vegetable oil
- 1 onion, chopped
- 2 cloves garlic, minced
- 2 carrots, peeled and sliced
- 2 celery stalks, sliced
- 2 potatoes, peeled and diced
- 2 cups chicken or vegetable broth
- 1 cup dry white wine (optional)
- 2 bay leaves
- 1 teaspoon dried thyme
- Salt and pepper, to taste
- Chopped fresh parsley, for garnish (optional)

Instructions:

1. Heat the oil in a large Dutch oven or heavy-bottomed pot over medium-high heat. Add the rabbit pieces and cook until browned on all sides, about 5-7 minutes. Remove the rabbit from the pot and set aside.
2. In the same pot, add the chopped onion and cook until softened and translucent, about 3-4 minutes. Add the minced garlic and cook for an additional minute.
3. Add the sliced carrots, celery, and diced potatoes to the pot. Stir to combine with the onions and garlic.
4. Return the browned rabbit pieces to the pot. Pour in the chicken or vegetable broth and dry white wine (if using). Add the bay leaves and dried thyme. Season with salt and pepper to taste.
5. Bring the stew to a simmer, then reduce the heat to low. Cover the pot and let the stew simmer gently for about 1 to 1 1/2 hours, or until the rabbit is tender and cooked through, and the vegetables are soft.
6. Taste the stew and adjust seasoning with salt and pepper, if needed.
7. Once the rabbit is tender, remove the bay leaves from the pot.
8. Serve the rabbit stew hot, garnished with chopped fresh parsley if desired.

Enjoy this comforting and flavorful rabbit stew with crusty bread or over cooked rice for a satisfying meal! Feel free to customize the recipe by adding your favorite herbs, spices, or additional vegetables.

Sauerbraten

Ingredients:

For the Marinade:

- 3-4 pounds beef roast (such as bottom round or chuck)
- 2 cups red wine vinegar
- 1 cup water
- 1 onion, thinly sliced
- 2 carrots, peeled and sliced
- 2 stalks celery, sliced
- 10 whole cloves
- 10 whole black peppercorns
- 2 bay leaves
- 1 tablespoon mustard seeds
- 1 tablespoon juniper berries
- 1 tablespoon brown sugar
- Salt and pepper, to taste

For Cooking:

- 2 tablespoons vegetable oil or lard
- 2 onions, sliced
- 2 tablespoons all-purpose flour
- 2 cups beef broth
- 1/4 cup brown sugar
- 1/4 cup red currant jelly (optional)
- Salt and pepper, to taste

Instructions:

1. In a large non-reactive container or resealable plastic bag, combine the red wine vinegar, water, sliced onion, sliced carrots, sliced celery, cloves, peppercorns, bay leaves, mustard seeds, juniper berries, brown sugar, salt, and pepper to make the marinade.

2. Place the beef roast in the marinade, making sure it is fully submerged. Seal the container or bag and refrigerate for 2-3 days, turning the meat occasionally to ensure even marinating.
3. After marinating, remove the beef roast from the marinade and pat it dry with paper towels. Strain the marinade and reserve the liquid, discarding the solids.
4. In a large Dutch oven or heavy-bottomed pot, heat the vegetable oil or lard over medium-high heat. Brown the beef roast on all sides, about 5 minutes per side. Remove the roast from the pot and set it aside.
5. Add the sliced onions to the pot and cook until softened and lightly caramelized, about 5-7 minutes.
6. Sprinkle the flour over the onions and cook, stirring constantly, for 1-2 minutes to make a roux.
7. Gradually add the reserved marinade liquid and beef broth to the pot, stirring to combine and scraping up any browned bits from the bottom of the pot.
8. Return the beef roast to the pot. Add the brown sugar and red currant jelly (if using). Season with salt and pepper to taste.
9. Bring the liquid to a simmer, then reduce the heat to low. Cover the pot and let the Sauerbraten simmer gently for 2-3 hours, or until the beef is tender and can be easily shredded with a fork.
10. Once the beef is cooked, remove it from the pot and let it rest for a few minutes before slicing.
11. Serve the Sauerbraten hot, sliced thinly, with the gravy spooned over the top.
12. Enjoy this flavorful and comforting German dish with traditional sides like potato dumplings, spaetzle, or red cabbage.

Sauerbraten is often served as a special dish for holidays or gatherings and is sure to be a hit with its rich and tangy flavors!

Shrimp Cocktail

Ingredients:

For the Shrimp:

- 1 pound large shrimp, peeled and deveined, tails intact
- 1 lemon, sliced
- 2 bay leaves
- Salt

For the Cocktail Sauce:

- 1/2 cup ketchup
- 2 tablespoons prepared horseradish
- 1 tablespoon fresh lemon juice
- 1 teaspoon Worcestershire sauce
- Tabasco sauce, to taste (optional)
- Salt and pepper, to taste

For Serving:

- Ice, for serving
- Lemon wedges, for serving
- Fresh parsley, for garnish (optional)

Instructions:

1. In a large pot, bring water to a boil. Add the sliced lemon, bay leaves, and a generous pinch of salt.
2. Once the water is boiling, add the shrimp to the pot and cook until they turn pink and are opaque, about 2-3 minutes. Be careful not to overcook the shrimp. They should be firm but still tender.
3. Using a slotted spoon, transfer the cooked shrimp to a bowl of ice water to stop the cooking process. Once cooled, drain the shrimp and pat them dry with paper towels.

4. In a small bowl, mix together the ketchup, prepared horseradish, fresh lemon juice, Worcestershire sauce, and Tabasco sauce (if using). Season the cocktail sauce with salt and pepper to taste.
5. Arrange the cooked shrimp on a serving platter or individual cocktail glasses filled with ice.
6. Serve the shrimp cocktail with the cocktail sauce on the side, along with lemon wedges for squeezing over the shrimp.
7. Garnish the shrimp cocktail with fresh parsley, if desired.
8. Enjoy this classic appetizer as a refreshing and flavorful start to your meal or as a light and elegant party snack!

Shrimp cocktail is simple to prepare yet always impressive with its vibrant colors and zesty flavors. It's perfect for entertaining or as a special treat for yourself!

Sole Veronique

Ingredients:

- 4 sole fillets (about 6 ounces each)
- Salt and pepper, to taste
- All-purpose flour, for dredging
- 2 tablespoons unsalted butter
- 1/2 cup dry white wine
- 1/2 cup fish or chicken broth
- 1/2 cup heavy cream
- 1 cup seedless green grapes, halved
- 1 tablespoon chopped fresh parsley
- Lemon wedges, for serving

Instructions:

1. Season the sole fillets with salt and pepper on both sides. Dredge each fillet lightly in flour, shaking off any excess.
2. In a large skillet, melt the butter over medium heat. Add the sole fillets to the skillet and cook for 2-3 minutes on each side, or until golden brown and cooked through. Remove the fillets from the skillet and transfer them to a plate. Cover loosely with foil to keep warm.
3. In the same skillet, deglaze with white wine, scraping up any browned bits from the bottom of the pan. Allow the wine to simmer for a minute or two to reduce slightly.
4. Stir in the fish or chicken broth and bring the mixture to a simmer. Let it cook for a few minutes until slightly reduced.
5. Reduce the heat to low and stir in the heavy cream. Simmer gently for another 2-3 minutes, stirring occasionally, until the sauce thickens slightly.
6. Add the halved grapes to the sauce and simmer for another minute to heat through.
7. Return the cooked sole fillets to the skillet, spooning some of the sauce and grapes over the top. Simmer for another minute or two to warm the fish through.
8. Sprinkle chopped fresh parsley over the sole Veronique just before serving.
9. Serve the sole Veronique hot, accompanied by lemon wedges for squeezing over the fish.

Enjoy this elegant and flavorful French dish, with its delicate fish, creamy sauce, and bursts of sweetness from the grapes! It's perfect for a special dinner party or romantic meal.

Steak Tartare

Ingredients:

- 8 ounces high-quality beef tenderloin or sirloin, finely minced or chopped
- 1 tablespoon Dijon mustard
- 1 tablespoon Worcestershire sauce
- 1 tablespoon capers, drained and chopped
- 1 tablespoon finely chopped shallots or red onion
- 1 tablespoon chopped fresh parsley
- 1 teaspoon cognac or brandy (optional)
- 1 teaspoon Tabasco sauce or hot sauce (optional)
- 1 egg yolk
- Salt and freshly ground black pepper, to taste
- Toasted bread or baguette slices, for serving

Instructions:

1. Start by ensuring that all utensils and surfaces used for preparing the Steak Tartare are clean and sanitized.
2. In a large mixing bowl, combine the finely minced or chopped beef with the Dijon mustard, Worcestershire sauce, chopped capers, chopped shallots or red onion, chopped parsley, cognac or brandy (if using), and Tabasco sauce or hot sauce (if using). Mix well to combine.
3. Season the mixture with salt and freshly ground black pepper to taste. Adjust the seasoning as needed.
4. Divide the mixture into individual portions and shape each portion into a mound on serving plates.
5. Create a small indentation in the center of each mound of beef and carefully place an egg yolk in each indentation.
6. Garnish the Steak Tartare with additional chopped parsley and capers, if desired.
7. Serve the Steak Tartare immediately with toasted bread or baguette slices on the side.
8. To eat, guests can mix the egg yolk into the beef mixture and spread it onto the toasted bread or baguette slices.

Enjoy this classic French dish as a sophisticated appetizer or light meal, perfect for entertaining or a special occasion. Remember to use the freshest and highest quality beef when making Steak Tartare, and always handle raw meat with care to ensure food safety.

Tarte Tatin

Ingredients:

For the Pastry:

- 1 1/4 cups all-purpose flour
- 1/2 teaspoon salt
- 1 tablespoon granulated sugar
- 1/2 cup unsalted butter, cold and cut into small cubes
- 3-4 tablespoons ice water

For the Apple Filling:

- 6-8 medium-sized apples (such as Granny Smith or Golden Delicious), peeled, cored, and halved
- 1/2 cup granulated sugar
- 1/4 cup unsalted butter
- 1 tablespoon lemon juice
- 1/2 teaspoon ground cinnamon (optional)

Instructions:

1. Preheat your oven to 375°F (190°C).
2. To make the pastry, in a large bowl, whisk together the flour, salt, and sugar. Add the cold cubed butter and use a pastry blender or your fingertips to cut the butter into the flour mixture until it resembles coarse crumbs.
3. Gradually add the ice water, 1 tablespoon at a time, mixing with a fork until the dough just comes together. Be careful not to overwork the dough. Shape the dough into a disk, wrap it in plastic wrap, and refrigerate it for at least 30 minutes.
4. While the dough is chilling, prepare the apple filling. In a 10-inch ovenproof skillet or Tarte Tatin pan, melt the butter over medium heat. Sprinkle the sugar evenly over the melted butter and cook, stirring occasionally, until the sugar is dissolved and starts to caramelize, about 5-7 minutes.
5. Remove the skillet from the heat and arrange the apple halves in the caramel, cut side down, in a circular pattern, fitting them snugly together.

6. Drizzle the lemon juice over the apples and sprinkle with ground cinnamon, if using.
7. Return the skillet to medium heat and cook the apples for 10-12 minutes, or until they start to soften and the caramel has thickened and darkened in color.
8. While the apples are cooking, roll out the chilled pastry dough on a lightly floured surface to fit the size of the skillet.
9. Once the apples are cooked, carefully place the pastry dough over the apples, tucking in the edges around the apples.
10. Transfer the skillet to the preheated oven and bake for 25-30 minutes, or until the pastry is golden brown and crisp.
11. Remove the skillet from the oven and let it cool for 5-10 minutes.
12. To serve, place a serving plate over the skillet and carefully invert the Tarte Tatin onto the plate, allowing the apples to fall onto the pastry. Be cautious as the caramel will be very hot.
13. Serve the Tarte Tatin warm, optionally with a scoop of vanilla ice cream or a dollop of whipped cream.

Enjoy this delicious and classic French dessert with its perfectly caramelized apples and buttery pastry!

Terrine de Foie Gras

Ingredients:

- 1 1/2 pounds (700g) fresh duck foie gras, cleaned and deveined
- 2 teaspoons salt
- 1/2 teaspoon freshly ground black pepper
- 1/4 teaspoon ground nutmeg
- 1/4 teaspoon ground cloves
- 1/4 cup (60ml) sweet wine, such as Sauternes or Port
- 1 tablespoon brandy or Cognac
- Sliced brioche or toasted bread, for serving
- Fleur de sel, for serving (optional)

Instructions:

1. Preheat your oven to 250°F (120°C).
2. Season the foie gras generously with salt, black pepper, nutmeg, and ground cloves. You can gently massage the seasoning into the foie gras to ensure even distribution.
3. In a shallow dish, place the seasoned foie gras and pour the sweet wine and brandy over it. Allow the foie gras to marinate in the wine mixture for about 30 minutes at room temperature.
4. After marinating, line a terrine mold or loaf pan with plastic wrap, leaving enough overhang to cover the top of the foie gras later.
5. Arrange the foie gras slices in the terrine mold, pressing them down gently to eliminate air pockets and create a smooth surface.
6. Fold the overhanging plastic wrap over the top of the foie gras to cover it completely.
7. Place the terrine mold in a larger baking dish or roasting pan and fill the outer dish with hot water to create a water bath (bain-marie).
8. Cover the entire setup with aluminum foil to prevent steam from escaping.
9. Bake the foie gras terrine in the preheated oven for about 45-60 minutes, or until the internal temperature reaches 120°F (49°C) on an instant-read thermometer.
10. Once cooked, remove the terrine mold from the water bath and let it cool to room temperature. Then, refrigerate the terrine for at least 24 hours to allow the flavors to develop and the terrine to set.

11. To serve, unmold the foie gras terrine by carefully lifting it out of the mold using the plastic wrap. Remove the plastic wrap and slice the terrine into thin slices.
12. Serve the Terrine de Foie Gras chilled or at room temperature, accompanied by sliced brioche or toasted bread. Optionally, sprinkle a pinch of fleur de sel over the foie gras slices before serving.

Enjoy this decadent and luxurious French delicacy as a special appetizer or part of a gourmet meal!

Tomato Aspic

Ingredients:

- 4 cups tomato juice
- 2 tablespoons unflavored gelatin
- 1/4 cup cold water
- 1/4 cup lemon juice
- 1 tablespoon Worcestershire sauce
- 1 teaspoon salt
- 1/2 teaspoon sugar
- 1/4 teaspoon ground black pepper
- Dash of hot sauce (optional)
- Chopped fresh herbs, such as parsley or basil, for garnish (optional)
- Thinly sliced vegetables or cooked shrimp, for garnish (optional)

Instructions:

1. In a small bowl, sprinkle the gelatin over the cold water and let it sit for 5 minutes to soften.
2. In a saucepan, heat the tomato juice over medium heat until hot but not boiling.
3. Add the softened gelatin to the hot tomato juice, stirring until completely dissolved.
4. Stir in the lemon juice, Worcestershire sauce, salt, sugar, black pepper, and hot sauce (if using). Taste and adjust seasoning as needed.
5. Remove the saucepan from the heat and let the mixture cool slightly.
6. Lightly grease a mold or individual serving dishes with non-stick cooking spray.
7. Pour the tomato mixture into the prepared mold or dishes.
8. Cover the mold or dishes with plastic wrap and refrigerate for at least 4 hours, or until the aspic is set.
9. To serve, dip the bottom of the mold or dishes in hot water for a few seconds to loosen the aspic. Invert the mold onto a serving platter or slide a knife around the edges of the dishes to release the aspic.
10. Garnish the tomato aspic with chopped fresh herbs and thinly sliced vegetables or cooked shrimp, if desired.
11. Serve the tomato aspic chilled as an appetizer or side dish.

Enjoy this refreshing and flavorful tomato aspic as a light and elegant addition to your meal! Feel free to customize the recipe by adding other ingredients like diced vegetables or herbs to suit your taste preferences.

Trout Almondine

Ingredients:

- 4 trout fillets (about 6-8 ounces each)
- Salt and pepper to taste
- 1/2 cup all-purpose flour
- 1/2 cup sliced almonds
- 4 tablespoons unsalted butter
- 2 tablespoons olive oil
- 2 tablespoons lemon juice
- 2 tablespoons chopped fresh parsley (optional)
- Lemon wedges for serving

Instructions:

1. Preheat the oven: Preheat your oven to 200°F (95°C) to keep the cooked trout warm while you prepare the sauce.
2. Season the trout: Season both sides of the trout fillets with salt and pepper. Dredge each fillet lightly in flour, shaking off any excess.
3. Toast the almonds: In a dry skillet over medium heat, toast the sliced almonds until they're lightly golden and fragrant. Be sure to watch them closely, as they can burn quickly. Once toasted, transfer them to a plate and set aside.
4. Cook the trout: In the same skillet, add 2 tablespoons of butter and 1 tablespoon of olive oil over medium-high heat. Once the butter is melted and sizzling, add the trout fillets, skin side down. Cook for about 3-4 minutes on each side until the fish is cooked through and the skin is crispy. Remove the trout from the skillet and transfer to an oven-safe dish. Keep warm in the preheated oven.
5. Make the sauce: In the same skillet, add the remaining butter and olive oil. Once the butter has melted, add the lemon juice and chopped parsley (if using). Cook for a minute or two until the sauce is heated through and slightly thickened.
6. Serve: Place the trout fillets on serving plates, spoon the almond butter sauce over the top, and sprinkle with the toasted almonds. Serve immediately with lemon wedges on the side.

Enjoy your Trout Almondine!

Veal Oscar

Ingredients:

- 4 veal scaloppine or medallions
- Salt and pepper to taste
- All-purpose flour, for dredging
- 2 tablespoons olive oil
- 8 asparagus spears, trimmed
- 8 ounces lump crabmeat, picked over for shells
- Béarnaise sauce (see recipe below)
- Fresh parsley, chopped (for garnish)
- Lemon wedges (for serving)

For the Béarnaise sauce:

- 3 egg yolks
- 1 tablespoon white wine vinegar
- 1 tablespoon water
- 1/2 cup unsalted butter, melted
- 1 tablespoon fresh tarragon, chopped
- Salt and pepper to taste

Instructions:

For the Béarnaise sauce:

1. Prepare a double boiler: Fill a saucepan with a couple of inches of water and bring it to a gentle simmer. Place a heatproof bowl over the saucepan, ensuring it doesn't touch the water.
2. Whisk egg yolks: In the bowl, whisk together the egg yolks, white wine vinegar, and water until well combined.
3. Slowly add butter: Gradually drizzle in the melted butter while continuously whisking the egg yolk mixture. Keep whisking until the sauce thickens and emulsifies, resembling a hollandaise sauce.
4. Add tarragon and season: Once the sauce has thickened, stir in the chopped tarragon. Season with salt and pepper to taste. Keep the sauce warm over the double boiler while you prepare the veal.

For the Veal Oscar:

1. Prepare the veal: Season the veal scaloppine with salt and pepper, then lightly dredge them in flour, shaking off any excess.

2. Cook the veal: In a large skillet, heat the olive oil over medium-high heat. Add the veal scaloppine and cook for 2-3 minutes on each side until they are golden brown and cooked through. Remove the veal from the skillet and set aside.
3. Cook the asparagus: In the same skillet, add the asparagus spears and cook until they are tender-crisp, about 3-4 minutes.
4. Assemble the Veal Oscar: Place the cooked veal on serving plates. Top each piece of veal with crabmeat and then arrange the asparagus spears on top. Spoon the Béarnaise sauce generously over the veal and asparagus.
5. Garnish and serve: Sprinkle chopped parsley over the Veal Oscar for a pop of color and freshness. Serve immediately with lemon wedges on the side.

Enjoy your decadent Veal Oscar!

Veal Piccata

Ingredients:

- 4 veal scaloppine (about 4-6 ounces each), pounded thin
- Salt and pepper to taste
- All-purpose flour, for dredging
- 2 tablespoons olive oil
- 2 tablespoons unsalted butter
- 1/3 cup dry white wine
- 1/2 cup chicken or vegetable broth
- Juice of 1 lemon
- 2 tablespoons capers, drained
- 2 tablespoons chopped fresh parsley (for garnish)
- Lemon slices (for serving)

Instructions:

1. Prepare the veal: Season the veal scaloppine with salt and pepper on both sides. Dredge each piece of veal in flour, shaking off any excess.
2. Cook the veal: In a large skillet, heat the olive oil and 1 tablespoon of butter over medium-high heat. Once hot, add the veal scaloppine to the skillet, making sure not to overcrowd the pan. Cook for 2-3 minutes on each side until they are golden brown and cooked through. Remove the veal from the skillet and transfer to a plate. Cover with foil to keep warm.
3. Make the sauce: In the same skillet, add the white wine and use a wooden spoon to scrape up any browned bits from the bottom of the pan. Let the wine simmer for a minute or two until it has reduced slightly.
4. Add broth, lemon juice, and capers: Pour in the chicken or vegetable broth and lemon juice. Add the capers to the skillet and stir to combine. Let the sauce simmer for another 2-3 minutes to thicken slightly.
5. Finish the sauce: Turn off the heat and swirl in the remaining tablespoon of butter until it's melted and incorporated into the sauce. Season the sauce with additional salt and pepper to taste if needed.
6. Serve: Place the cooked veal scaloppine on serving plates and spoon the sauce over the top. Garnish with chopped parsley and serve with lemon slices on the side.

Enjoy your delicious Veal Piccata with your favorite side dishes, such as pasta, rice, or roasted vegetables. Buon appetito!

Wiener Schnitzel

Ingredients:

- 4 veal cutlets (about 4-6 ounces each), pounded thin
- Salt and pepper to taste
- All-purpose flour, for dredging
- 2 large eggs
- 1 cup breadcrumbs (preferably fresh)
- Vegetable oil, for frying
- Lemon wedges, for serving
- Parsley sprigs, for garnish (optional)

Instructions:

1. Prepare the veal: Season the veal cutlets with salt and pepper on both sides.
2. Dredge the veal: Set up a breading station with three shallow dishes. Place the flour in the first dish, beat the eggs in the second dish, and put the breadcrumbs in the third dish. Dredge each veal cutlet in the flour, shaking off any excess, then dip it into the beaten eggs, and finally coat it evenly with breadcrumbs, pressing gently to adhere.
3. Heat the oil: In a large skillet, heat enough vegetable oil over medium-high heat to cover the bottom of the pan. You'll need about 1/4 inch of oil. To test if the oil is hot enough, drop a small breadcrumb into the oil; if it sizzles and floats to the top, the oil is ready.
4. Fry the veal: Carefully place the breaded veal cutlets into the hot oil, making sure not to overcrowd the pan. Fry the cutlets for 2-3 minutes on each side until they are golden brown and crispy. Depending on the size of your skillet, you may need to fry the cutlets in batches.
5. Drain and serve: Once the veal cutlets are cooked, transfer them to a plate lined with paper towels to drain any excess oil.
6. Serve: Serve the Wiener Schnitzel immediately while it's still hot, garnished with lemon wedges and parsley sprigs if desired. Traditionally, Wiener Schnitzel is served with potato salad, cucumber salad, or lingonberry jam on the side.

Enjoy your homemade Wiener Schnitzel, a true taste of Austrian cuisine!

Yorkshire Pudding

Ingredients:

- 1 cup all-purpose flour
- 1 cup milk
- 2 large eggs
- 1/2 teaspoon salt
- Vegetable oil, beef drippings, or melted butter for greasing the pan

Instructions:

1. Preheat the oven: Preheat your oven to 425°F (220°C). Place a Yorkshire pudding tin or muffin tin in the oven to heat up while you prepare the batter.
2. Make the batter: In a mixing bowl, whisk together the flour, milk, eggs, and salt until you have a smooth batter with no lumps. The consistency should be similar to pancake batter. Let the batter rest for about 30 minutes at room temperature. This allows the flour to fully absorb the liquid and helps the Yorkshire puddings puff up.
3. Prepare the pan: Once the oven is preheated and the pan is hot, carefully remove it from the oven. Add a small amount of vegetable oil, beef drippings, or melted butter to each cup of the tin, filling them about halfway.
4. Pour the batter: Quickly pour the batter into the hot cups of the tin, filling each one about two-thirds full.
5. Bake: Place the tin back into the oven and bake the Yorkshire puddings for 20-25 minutes, or until they are puffed up and golden brown.
6. Serve: Remove the Yorkshire puddings from the oven and serve them immediately while they're still hot and puffy. They make a delicious accompaniment to roast beef and gravy, but they can also be enjoyed with other roast meats or as part of a vegetarian meal.

Enjoy your homemade Yorkshire puddings as a classic addition to your Sunday roast or any special meal!

www.ingramcontent.com/pod-product-compliance
Lightning Source LLC
LaVergne TN
LVHW062047070526
838201LV00080B/2129